WWII Bakelite Jewelry

Love & Victory

Bambi Deville Engeran

Schiffer Publishing Ltd
4880 Lower Valley Road • Atglen, PA • 19310

Items are from the collection of
Bambi Deville Engeran

Photography and design are by
Nijme Rinaldi-Nun, Maija Beeton, Leslie Collom and
Bambi Deville Engeran

Three-color, single-star, badge pin,

Big Ben with Tank Pin,

Three-color, laminated, Victory Pin with emblem

Other Schiffer Books on Related Subjects:
Star Spangled Jewelry. Sandra J. Whitson
Antique Sweetheart Jewelry. Nicholas D. Snider

Library of Congress Control Number: 2011936165

Designed by Danielle D. Farmer
Cover Design by Bruce Waters
Type set in Goudy Handtooled/Goudy Old Style/Zurich BT

ISBN: 978-0-7643-3871-7

Printed in China

Published by Schiffer Publishing Ltd.
4880 Lower Valley Road
Atglen, PA 19310
Phone: (610) 593-1777; Fax: (610) 593-2002
E-mail: Info@schifferbooks.com

In Europe, Schiffer books are distributed by
Bushwood Books
6 Marksbury Ave.
Kew Gardens
Surrey TW9 4JF England
Phone: 44 (0) 20 8392 8585; Fax: 44 (0) 20 8392 9876
E-mail: info@bushwoodbooks.co.uk
Website: www.bushwoodbooks.co.uk

Patriotic tassel pin with eagle

Dedication

To the troops who we love and appreciate.
To the loved ones who kept home fires burning.
To the National WWII Museum in New Orleans, its patrons and supporters.

Bluebirds Carry Love Notes necklace and detail

"There will be Bluebirds over the White Cliffs of Dover" are the lyrics to one of the most popular songs of 1942. The most famous version of the song was sung by British artist Vera Lynn. Bluebirds flying love notes are depicted in this necklace. It was a song of hope for the British people who were fighting Germany. Love notes are being carried to sweethearts.

Credits

The WWII newspaper headlines are part of the extensive and wonderful WWII artifacts collection of Dr. David Mermelloid, DDS. The self-portraits shown in this book are by artist, model and photographer Leslie Collom, of Houma, Louisiana.

All photographs in this book are the sole property of the author, with the exception of the White Cliffs of Dover. Dramatic Sky Over the White Cliffs of Dover copyright Dennis Dolkens/dreamtime.com; A picture of the dramatic sky over the white cliffs of Dover, in England, was taken on July 7th, 2010.

Jewelry photography by Nijme.com.
Digital art in chapter 10 is by Maija Beeton.
Author's portrait is by Mario Didonato.

The content and editorial concepts presented in this book are solely those of the author, who bears complete responsibility for them; especially those which are considered politically incorrect.

Several pieces from the author's collection have been featured in both films and magazine editorials.

Contents

Preface

Being a collectibles dealer means I get to shop for Bakelite all day, every day. It also enables me to devote time to my writing, performing, cooking, family, and to my pets, the other joys in my life. Creating this personal collection of WWII-era Bakelite jewelry has been ongoing for years. I am thrilled to have an opportunity to share it with you.

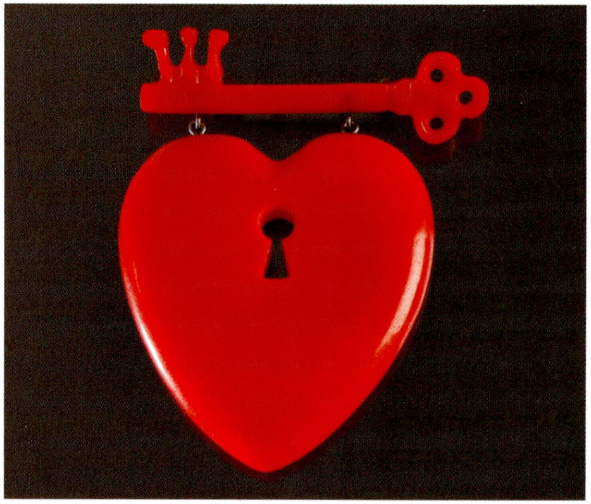

Oversized Key-to-my-heart pin

People always ask me how I started collecting Bakelite. The real question is "How did I start collecting?" To be fair, my mother and father were both antiques collectors: music boxes, stamps, coins, art, jewelry, books, furniture, Depression glass—the list goes on. I knew we dined on Queen Anne chairs and watched *Lost in Space* from a Louis 14th couch. Everything in the house had a history and a story. Collecting, for me, became an interest in another time, in history.

For my specific interest in vintage jewelry, I have my two grandmothers to thank. First, Grandma Anna, my father's mother, who, with my Grandfather Engeran, owned a bar and a casino in New Orleans in the 1940s and 1950s. The Old Loyalty on Rampart Street is now the home of The New Orleans Jazz and Heritage Festival Foundation. My grandmother, Mumsy we called her, had the glamour and style of a movie star. She always said she dressed well because she could then go anywhere on a whim, with anyone. This included flying to New York to The Cotton Club and dancing in Cuba, on a moment's notice. She was a dramatic, fun woman.

I was lucky enough to be the only one of my five sisters who was not petite. Like Grandma Anna, I was tall and voluptuous, which meant I was able to wear her fabulous gowns and dresses. One day, which I still remember, at age 13, while helping her clean her storage, a dozen or so hats from her closet toppled onto my head. Wasn't I thrilled to learn there were shoes that fit me perfectly and then the discovery of her jewels? I still have the first necklace and earring set Grandma gave me. I was smitten with another era. She told me I reminded her of Thelma Todd.

This was the beginning of the glamorous life! I started accumulating anything I could find from the era and also became interested in the films and music of the time.

On the other side of Lake Ponchartrain, my Grandma Deville, my mother's mother, lived. Grandma Deville was the antitheses of Grandma Anna. She grew up in the country and was very practical. She was a firm believer in a young man serving his country and always wore her American Flag on her chest. An American flag had a permanent home in front of their house, and family portraits of those who served were exhibited in every room.

Grandma spoke often of her brother, Andrew, lost at the battle of Normandy. My grandfather Deville held office in the Louisiana State Legislature, which was how he served his country. Both of my uncles, my mother's two brothers, were in the military. I am proud of my sister Laura, who is currently a captain and nurse practitioner in the U.S. Army. Grandma Deville was never without her American flag pins—her red, white, and blue jewels. Wearing her patriotic jewelry reminded Grandma of her brothers. This brings me to how I started collecting Bakelite jewelry.

I was an acting student living in New York City at the age of eighteen. An interest in vintage jewelry was infused by the discovery of the now-defunct 26th Street flea market. I would go every Sunday with very little money to spend on a found treasure. I would find a dress for five dollars or a piece of jewelry, usually rhinestones or early Haskell. When I met my soon-to-be husband, David, I found out quickly that we shared a passion for vintage watches. We discovered clocks, then clock radios and eventually the magnificent Bakelite and Catalan radios. I soon discovered a little shop in the east village on Thompson Street, near the old Betsy Johnson clothing store, that had jewelry made of the same material. And, contrary to popular belief, it was very expensive. I could not afford to buy any of this beautiful jewelry. No matter, I would go back and study the collection, hoping to come across a piece at the flea market. Well, that never happened. However, I did accumulate a nice simple bangle collection in the beginning; until my now-former husband traded my bracelets for a radio he wanted. As I started to save money I began my collection. A few years later I discovered my first "Sweetheart" pin. Then I found a little sailor, then a flag pin....Like Grandma's butt made of Bakelite. This was fun. And so I focused. "That's the story morning glory!" as my Aunt Jackie would say. I turned a hobby into a business really out of shear love and the passion to always follow my heart.

In 1941 the world was at war. It was common knowledge that metals were to be reserved for the war effort. In fact, Conservation Order M-162 prohibited the use of platinum and iridium for jewelry. Jewelers then turned to Bakelite, which had been gaining popularity since the Great Depression.

Acknowledgements

Maija Beeton has been an incredible source of inspiration and assistance, without whose help this would have been a very different experience. Gratitude also goes to Andre Bustanoby, who loaned me his wife. Equally unparalleled in their support were great friends and artists Leslie Collom, for her self-portraits and Michael Fedor for his insights and expertise in regards to my interest in art history. Nijme Rinaldi-Nun, my primary jewelry photographer, for her hard work. Mara Mikialian, thank you! My dentist, Dr. David Mermelloid, many thanks for loaning his wonderful WWII Headlines Collection. Much love and support was given by friends Diana Lewinstein and Madalyn Irell. Gratitude to Caroline Somers, Marion White and Julia Adams and Anita Stern of This and That Collectibles in New York City, fellow Bakelite ladies; my sister, great chef and BFF Christiane Engeran, who I owe a Margarita, deserves a nod as well. Alexandra Monett is a wonderful friend and valuable woman in the Arts for many years, thank you; Lucille Tempesta exposed me to the world of vintage jewelry collecting on a level I was thrilled to discover; I thank my editor, Nancy Schiffer, for her belief in this project; and Joseph Langman at Schiffer Publishing for his encouragement;. Thanks to my father, Lloyd Engeran, Jr., for his support, and for my little angel, Heidi Felene, who misses her Mamma. I do not use the words "friend" or "love" lightly, which is why, in the final hour, I have been able to count on them both.

Waiting is the Pits with Cherries

Heart Pin, My Honey is a Flyer Pin,

Sweetheart Heart Pin with Emblem.

Introduction

The curatorial choices for the jewelry shown in this book reflect the incredible passion women of this period held for their loved ones overseas. This jewelry was a way to literally wear your sentiment. The longing for your true love was where the passion lay. The knowledge that he was fighting for you and your family, and the possibility of spending your life together, was the driving force. Love, passion, romance and patriotism were themes to live by. The most powerful aspect that began my interest in the WWII era jewelry is the sentiment, the love and passion brought about when studying a Bakelite piece from this era. It is so romantic knowing that a woman who wore one of these pieces was waiting for a loved one to return from abroad. The cultural significance of this jewelry is profound. Unlike having a lock of his hair hidden under a pillow, the women wore their hearts on their sleeves, their necks and their bosoms. The sacrifices were mutual. For many soldiers, their devotion was shown in the form of tattoos with their wife's name on their arm and, of course, 'MOTHER'. The manifestation of a "Sweetheart" pin on a woman's lapel was her proclaiming, "My special guy is away, I will wait for him." How wonderful to feel that kind of passion for another human being.

Three pins: American Flag Pin, Uncle Sam Pin, Yankees 1941 Baseball Pin

PATRIOTISM

Then conquer we must, for our cause it is just and this be our motto, In God is our trust.
And the star spangled banner in triumph shall wave 'oar the land of the free and the home of the brave'.

CHAPTER 1

PATRIOTISM

American
Flag Pin

Three-color, decorative necklace with seven pennants

CHAPTER 1

PATRIOTISM

Three-color shield pin with eagle and star

Rounded and elongated eagle pin in three colors

Don't Tread on
Me snake pin

Shield pin with
single star

CHAPTER 1

PATRIOTISM

Dog with patriotic ball pin

Five-color, Philadelphia style necklace with six flags

Red Victory pin with gold Marine symbol

Three-color patriotic bar pin with thirteen stars

CHAPTER 1

PATRIOTISM

USA star and three-color heart pin

Uncle Sam large hat pin

USA map pin
in three colors

Group of
three pins

Large Red
Star bib
necklace

CHAPTER 1

PATRIOTISM

Three-color, carved eagle pin

USA map in three colors with Marine crest

Apple juice, USA, disc necklace with tassels and blue link chain

Patriotic
tassel pin
with eagle

CHAPTER
1

PATRIOTISM

Elongated eagle pin in three colors with beveled edges

Three-color, striped, shield pin with star

Necklace with blue link chain and six squares with Marine Corps emblem

Three-color, layered and laminated red heart with Marine Corps emblem

CHAPTER 1

PATRIOTISM

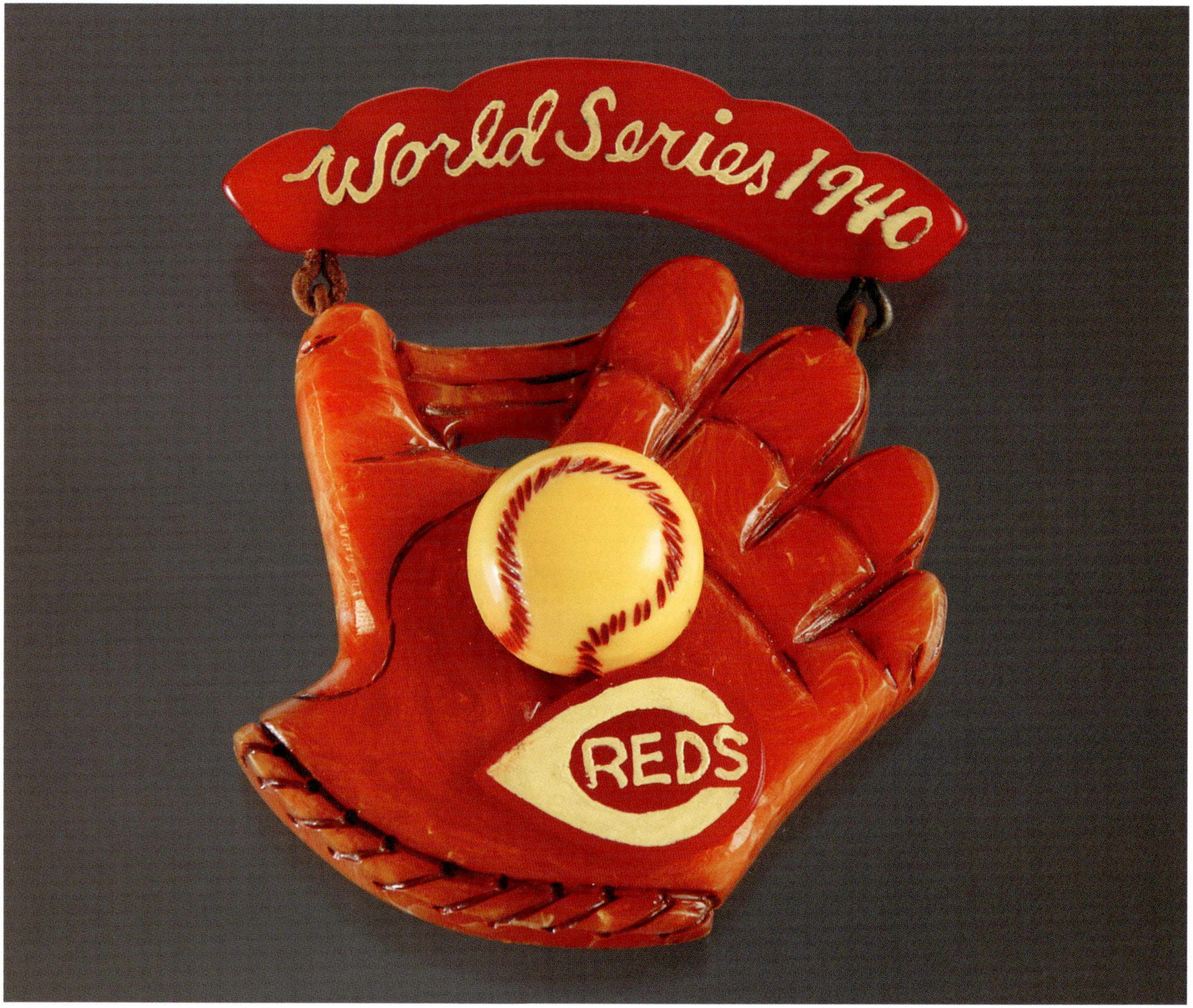

"World Series 1940" baseball pin with glove, ball and REDS insignia

In 1941, major league baseball was more popular than ever. In 1942 there were fears that the war would jeopardize this popular sport. Because of the military draft, baseball lost its first two players who entered military service. President Roosevelt, in response to a direct plea from baseball's ruling head, Kenesaw Mountain Landis, sent

"Yankees 1941" World Series heart pin with flag, glove and ball

his now-famous, January 15, "Green Light" letter. Roosevelt also noted that baseball could provide entertainment for at least twenty million people, and added that although the quality of the teams might be lowered by using different players replacing young men going into military service, this would not infringe upon the popularity of the sport.

After seeing the film *A League of Their Own*, the author became aware of the All American Girl's Baseball League. In 1943, President Roosevelt urged Mr. Wrigley, the owner of the Chicago Cubs, to keep baseball going. The women's league was started and scouts were hired to find the best players. The best also included the most beautiful, and the ladies attended charm school and were given professional beauty makeovers.

CHAPTER 1

PATRIOTISM

Bar pin with "Loose Lips Sink Ships, Button Up"

The original phrase, "Loose lips might sink ships," was coined during WWII as part of the U.S, Office of War Information Department's attempt to limit the possibility of people giving information to enemy spies. More information is available at *www.eyewitnesstohistory.com*.

Navy anchor and lifesavers necklace on braided cord, and pin with sailor's hat and Navy anchor

I LOVE A SAILOR

CHAPTER 2

I LOVE A SAILOR

Black heart inscribed "Pearl Harbor 12-7-41" with anchor, memorial pin

Navy anchor and lifesavers necklace on braided cord

"Sweetheart in Service" pin with red anchor and blue disc

Sambo as a sailor pin with googley eyes

Sailor pin with linked sleeves and yellow pants

Red cord necklace with five anchors

CHAPTER 2

I LOVE A SAILOR

Pin of two blue anchors with a red heart charm and Military insignia

Necklace of metal chain with four heart and anchor charms

CHAPTER 2

I LOVE A SAILOR

"Husband"
with anchor
on heart pin

Bar pin with white sailor's cap and black pendant anchor

Sailor pin with linked sleeves and blue pants

Navy blue anchor pin wrapped with metal chain

CHAPTER 2

I LOVE A SAILOR

"Sweetheart in Service" pin with red anchor and a blue disc and necklace of metal chain with four heart and anchor charms

Red heart pin with
metal anchor

"I love A US
Sailor" arrow
and anchor pin

Sailor pin with linked sleeves
and blue pants

CHAPTER
2

I LOVE A SAILOR

"Sweetheart" arrow pin with golden rope and anchor on red heart

Ten red, white and blue anchor charms on a necklace of metal chain

CHAPTER
2

I LOVE A SAILOR

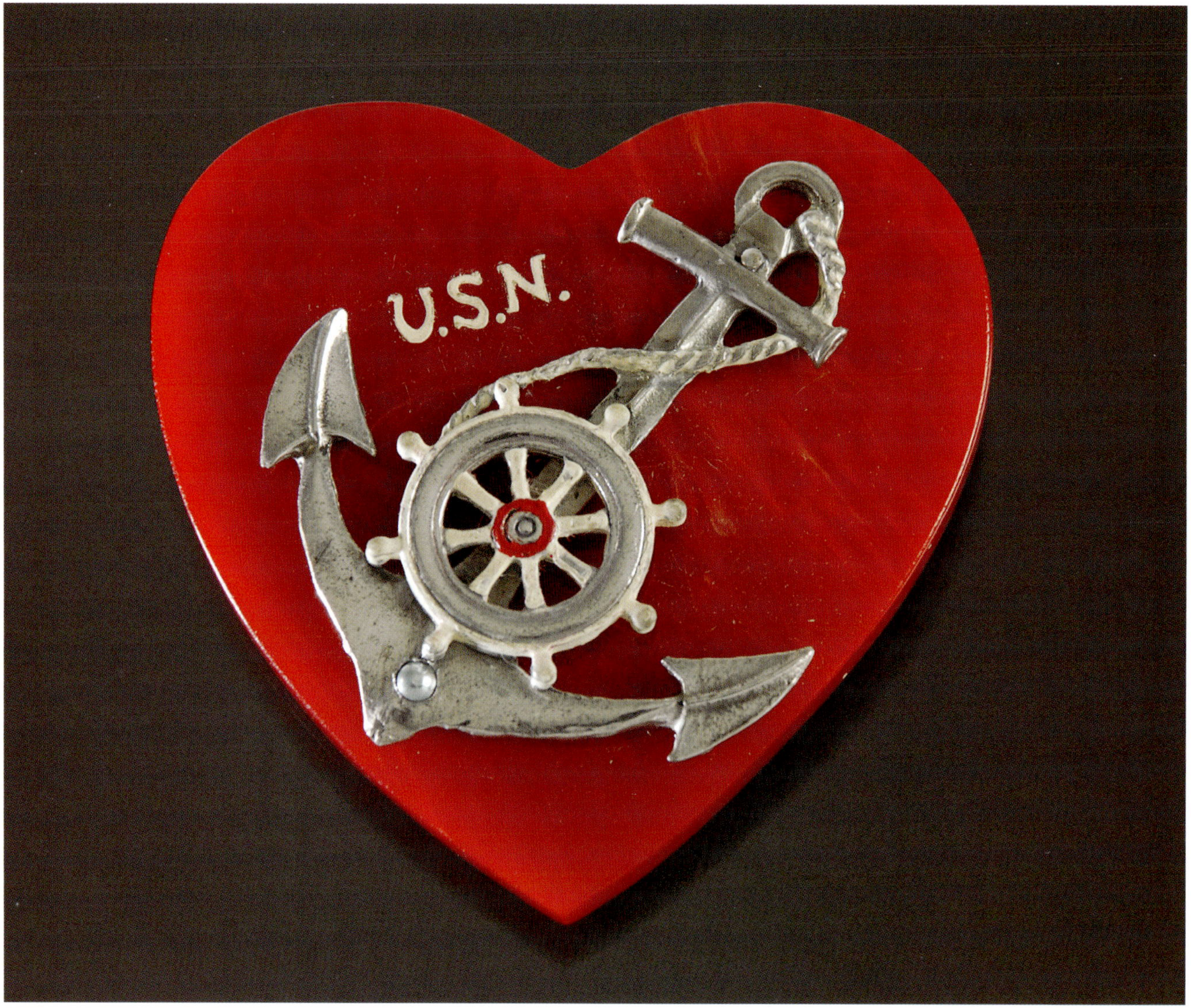

"U.S.N." on marbleized red heart pin with golden anchor, rope and wheel

Sambo pin and anchor pin with newspaper headline

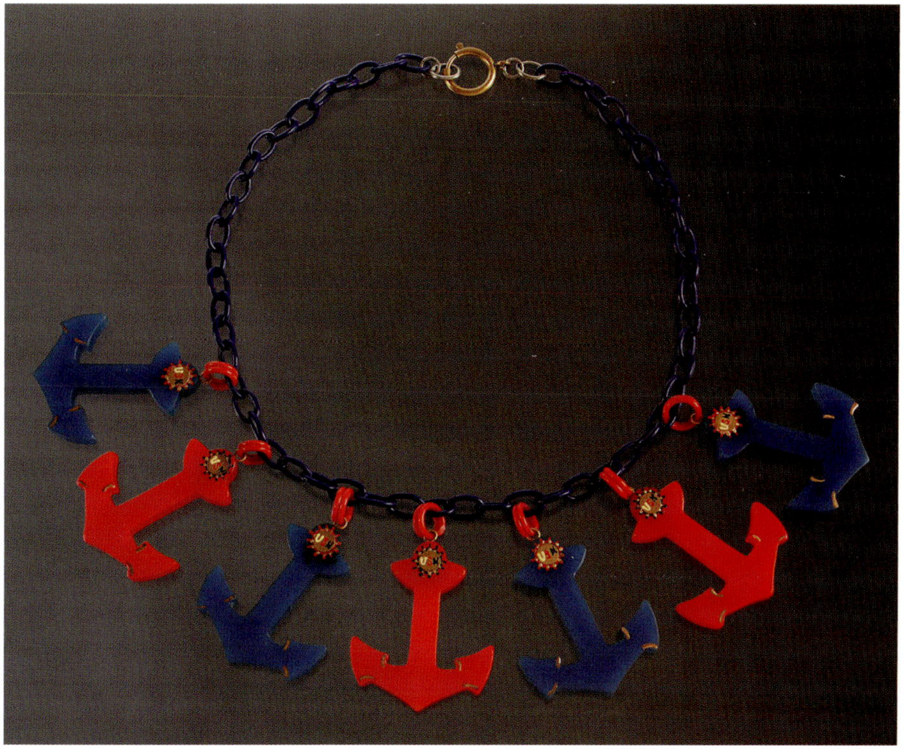

Seven red and blue anchor charms on a blue cord necklace, with "USN" on metal discs

CHAPTER 2

I LOVE A SAILOR

Red cuff bracelet with metal anchors on blue and white squares

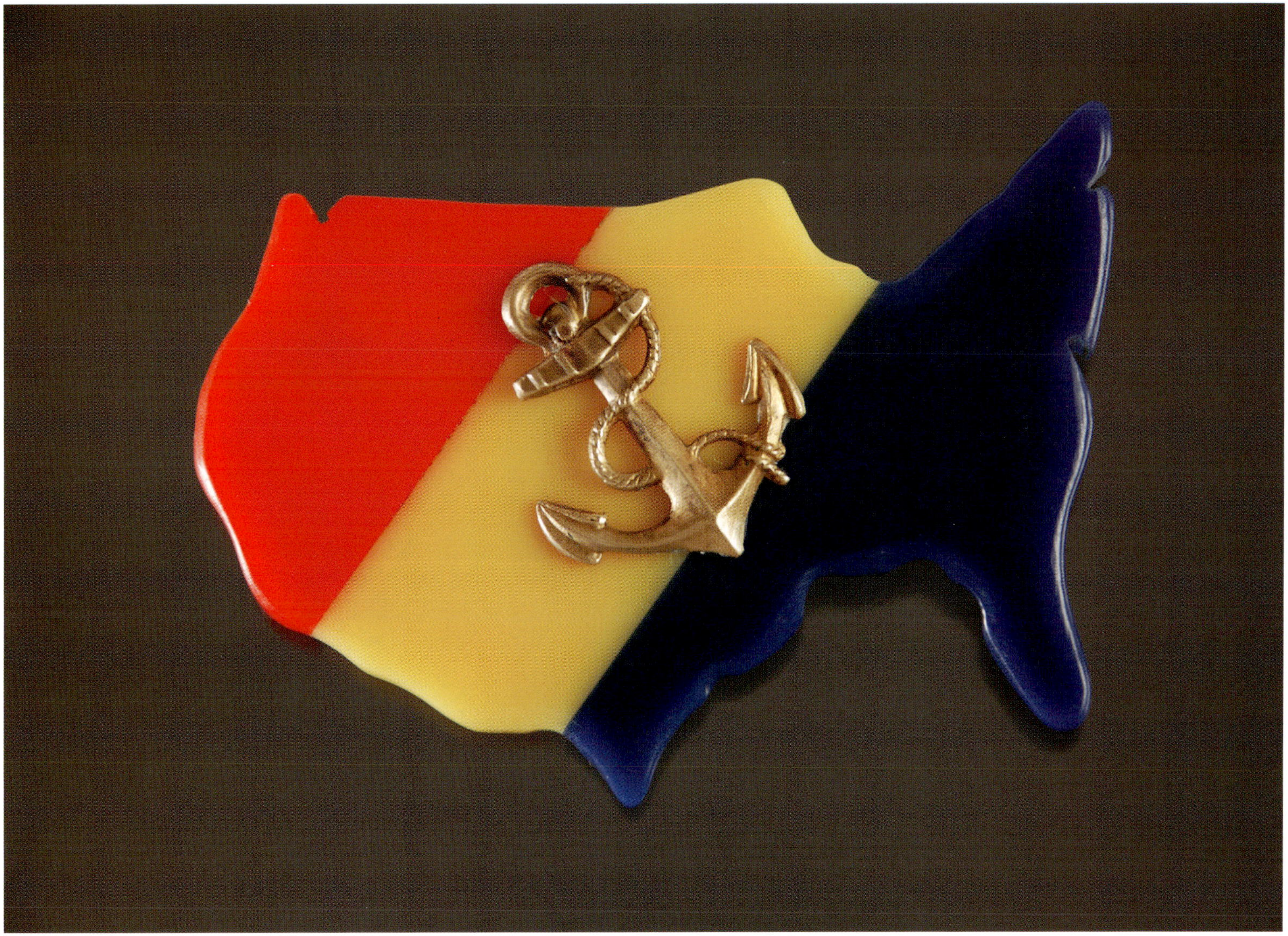

Tri-color U.S.
map pin with
metal anchor

CHAPTER 2

I LOVE A SAILOR

Three-color heart with "V" for Victory pin

Tortoise shell colored round charm with embossed metal tank

Large, googley-eyed, U.S. Army mule pin Olive green

"Sweetheart" pin with metal tank design

ROLL IN THE TROOPS

Small, jointed, soldier pin with linked arms and legs

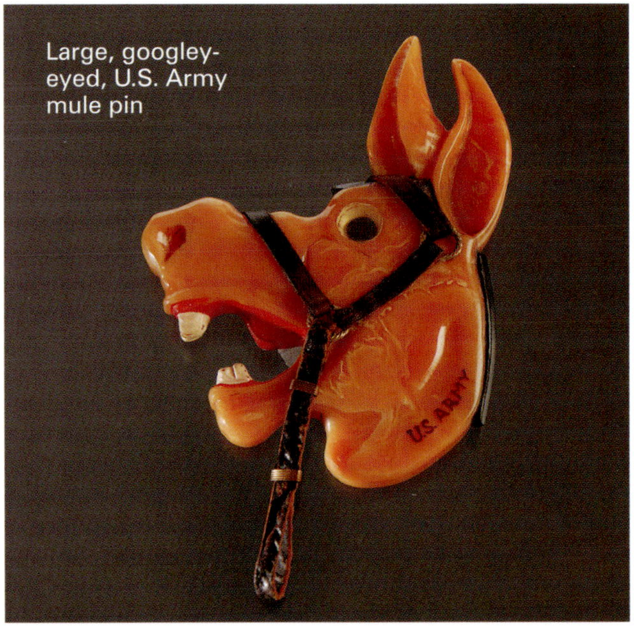

Large, googley-eyed, U.S. Army mule pin

Seven officer's rank charms

Navy blue Eiffel Tower with a tank pin

Six red disc charms with metal tank designs

Olive green "Sweetheart" pin with metal tank design

Jointed soldier pin with linked arms and legs

A red disc charm with metal tank design

Jointed soldier pin with linked arms and legs

Navy blue Eiffel Tower with a tank pin

Big Ben with a metal tank pin

Three-color bar pin with a red heart and metal tank

Necklace of knotted black cord and ten red bugles

This necklace design is based on a song from the film *Buck Privates*, titled "Boogie Woogie Bugle Boy of Company B," that was written by Don Raye and Hughie Prince and recorded in Hollywood in 1941. It was nominated for an Academy Award for Best Song, The film depicts a street musician who was drafted into the U.S. Army during the Roosevelt administration's wartime draft and allowed to play reveille, accompanied by other musicians "eight to the bar."

Three-color laminated island pin with a palm tree and officer's hat

Necklace of a blue link chain and six striped flags

In 1941, General Douglas MacArthur was recalled to command U.S. and Filipino troops defending the Philippine Islands against Japanese aggression. MacArthur's troops fought a stubborn, strategic withdrawal, holding out at Bataan and Corregidor until May of 1942. MacArthur left for Australia in February, with the famous pledge: "I came through and I shall return." As the Supreme Allied Commander in the southwest Pacific, he planned the Pacific offensive that was launched in the autumn of 1942, following the massive naval and air battles at Midway Island in June. Coordinating air cover, naval bombardment, and amphibious landings, General MacArthur embarked on a strategy of island hopping, capturing the smaller islands and bypassing those that were larger and more heavily defended. In October of 1944, General MacArthur commenced the reconquest of the Philippines, and on the fourth of February, 1945, U.S. troops entered Manila. General MacArthur's command was extended to all U.S. Army forces in the Pacific area. It was MacArthur who accepted the Japanese surrender on September 2, 1945, following the explosion of U.S. atomic bombs at Hiroshima and Nagasaki.

Multiple-color necklace with four airplanes and flying aces pilots with moveable heads

"USA Army" airplane on a 3-color bar pin

Allied airplane pin "To Adolph From FDR" Bullet Pin

LOOK OUT BELOW

CHAPTER 4

LOOK OUT BELOW

Multiple-color necklace with four airplanes and flying aces pilots with moveable heads

"USA Army" airplane on a 3-color bar pin

Flying ace pin

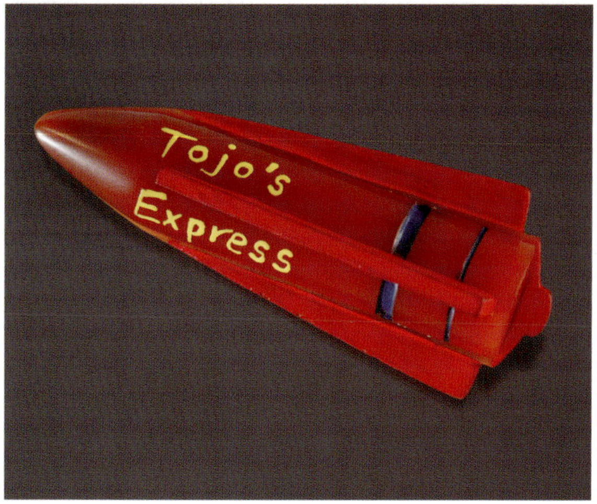

"Tojo's Express" torpedo pin

CHAPTER 4

LOOK OUT BELOW

"A A F - Army" bomber pin	Bar pin with bomb pendants: "Hitler Stalin Benito"	"Hey Jap, You're Next" bullet pin	"Remember Pearl Harbor" red bullet pin	"Tojo's Express" torpedo pin	"Hitler Stalin Mussolini Tojo" bombs bar pin

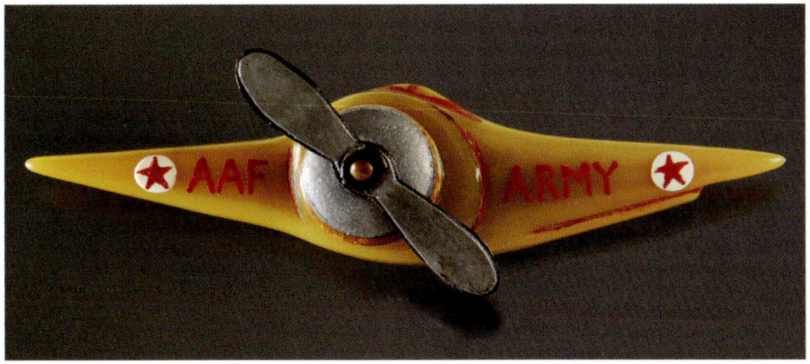

"A A F - Army" bomber pin

Red heart pin with "My Honey's a Flyer" and metal airplane

"Hitler Stalin
Mussolini Tojo"
bombs bar pin

"Remember Pearl Harbor" red bullet pin
"Give 'em Hell" red bullet pin
"Hey Jap, You're Next" red bullet pin

CHAPTER 4

LOOK OUT BELOW

Standing officer pin | Army Air Corps bomber necklace with clouds

Army Air Corps
bomber necklace
with clouds

Hitler-Stalin-
Mussolini-Tojo
torpedo pin

CHAPTER 4

LOOK OUT BELOW

Allied airplane pin

US Army Air Corps necklace with red, white and blue link chain, three three-propellar charms, and two three-color flag charms

"Remember Pearl Harbor" torpedo pin,

LOOK OUT BELOW

Three-color laminated island pin with a palm tree and officer's hat

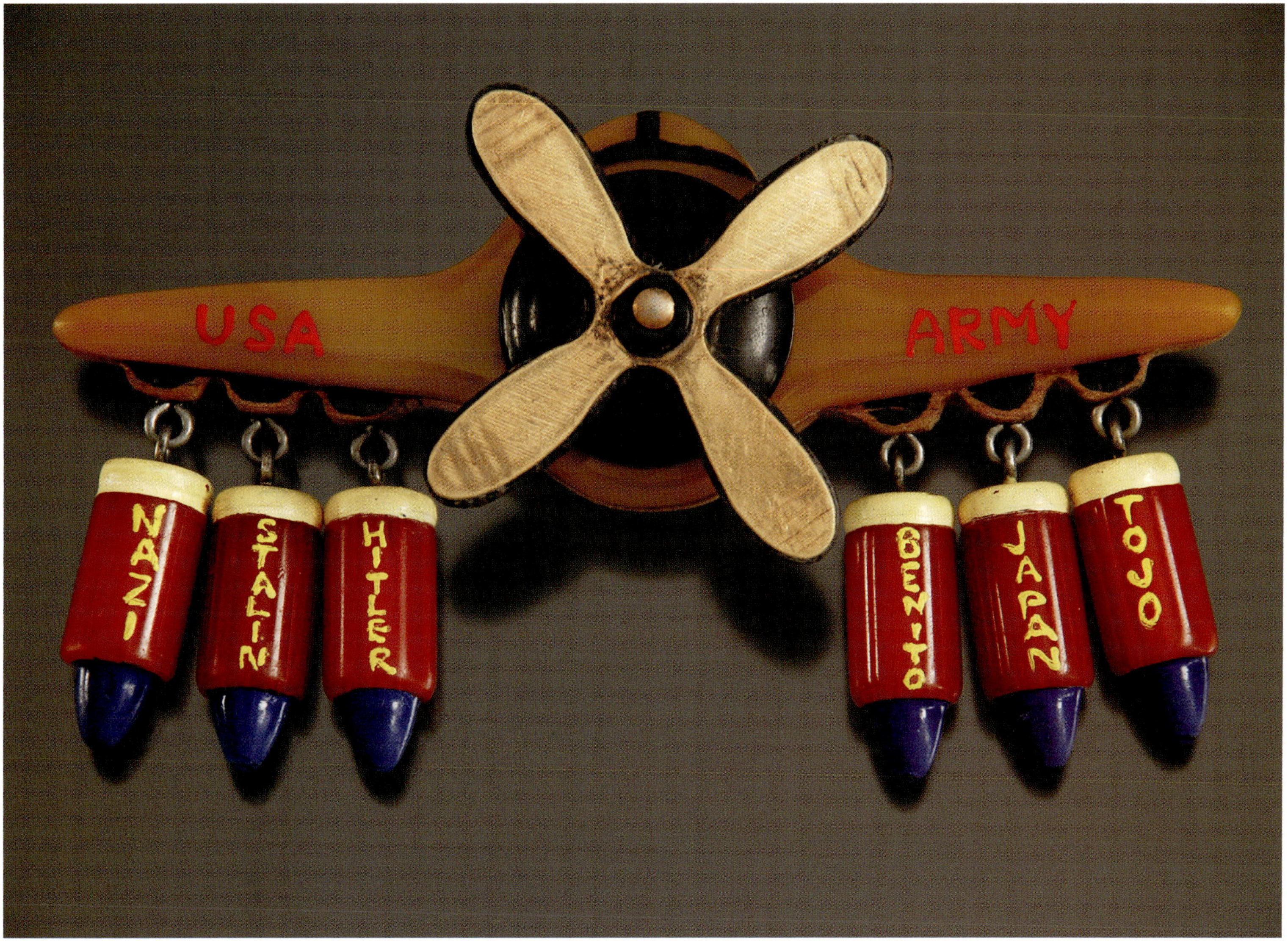

Pin of airplane wings and propeller and six bombs marked: Nazi, Stalin, Hitler, Benito, Japan, Tojo

CHAPTER 4

LOOK OUT BELOW

Necklace of blue knotted cord and three charms of airplanes

The Flying Tigers was the nickname for an American volunteer group originally commanded by Major John Chemault. The Tigers raised the spirits of Americans surrounding the war effort. The 'War Hawks' group went into action over Burma on December 20, 1941.

Bar pin with red heart charm inscribed "Waiting is the pits" and two cherries

Red heart pin inscribe "My Honey's a Flyer" with metal airplane

Red heart pin with silver metal "Sweetheart" and insignia

SWEETHEARTS

CHAPTER 5

SWEETHEARTS

Link chain necklace with five red hearts inscribed "Sweetheart"

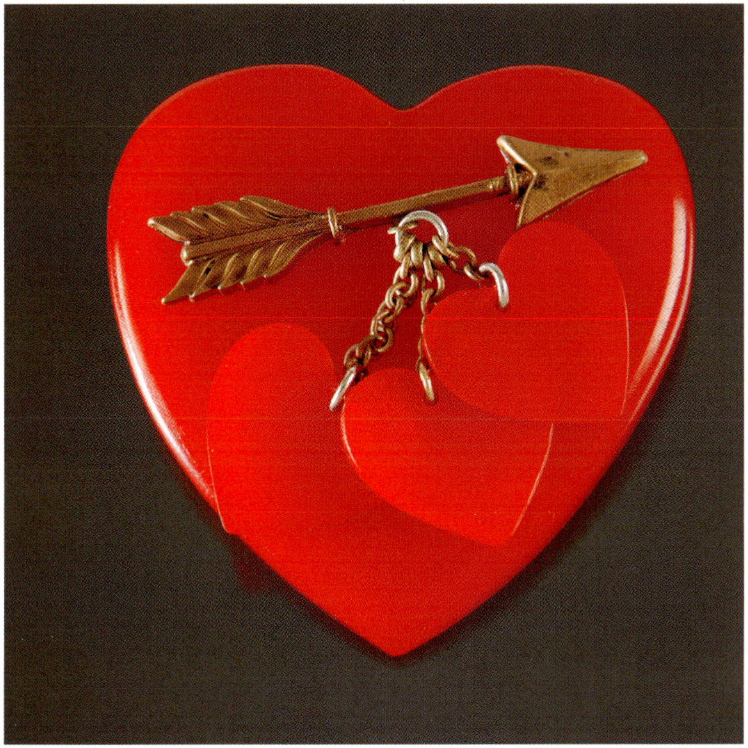

Red heart-shaped pin with three heart charms and a metal arrow

Extra large, three-color bar pin with metal "Sweetheart" and charms of hearts and love letters marked "Son," "Lover," "Hubby," "Uncle," "Brother"

CHAPTER 5

SWEETHEARTS

Large red heart with arrow pin

Green bar pin with a hanging metal tank design

Striped heart pin with metal "Sweetheart"

Layered heart pin with metal "Sweet heart"

Red, white and blue link necklace with four blue and three striped signal flag charms

Red heart pin
with metal
"Sweetheart" and
military insignia

Dark red
heart pin with
golden metal
"Sweetheart"

CHAPTER 5

SWEETHEARTS

Extra large, three-color bar pin with metal "Sweetheart" and charms of hearts and love letters marked "Son," "Lover," "Hubby," "Uncle," "Brother"

Red pin with golden metal "Sweetheart" and six red crystal dangles

Necklace or bracelet with four striped hearts and metal anchor insignia

CHAPTER 5

SWEETHEARTS

Layered red heart pin with "Husband" and golden metal anchor

Metal chain necklace with three pink and metal heart charms and four red heart and metal lock charms attached

Black link necklace with five red heart charms, each with a black-framed, apple juice glass gem

Three red heart pins with golden metal "Sweetheart" applied

Layered red heart pin with applied "V"

CHAPTER 5

SWEETHEARTS

Red link necklace with three yellow heart charms

Layered red heart pin with "Husband" and golden metal anchor

Necklace or bracelet with four striped hearts and metal anchor insignia

Bar pin "Sweetheart in Service" with pendant blue disc and red anchor

CHAPTER 5

SWEETHEARTS

Black heart inscribed "Pearl Harbor 12-7-41" with anchor, memorial pin

Red heart pin with golden metal "Sweetheart" applied

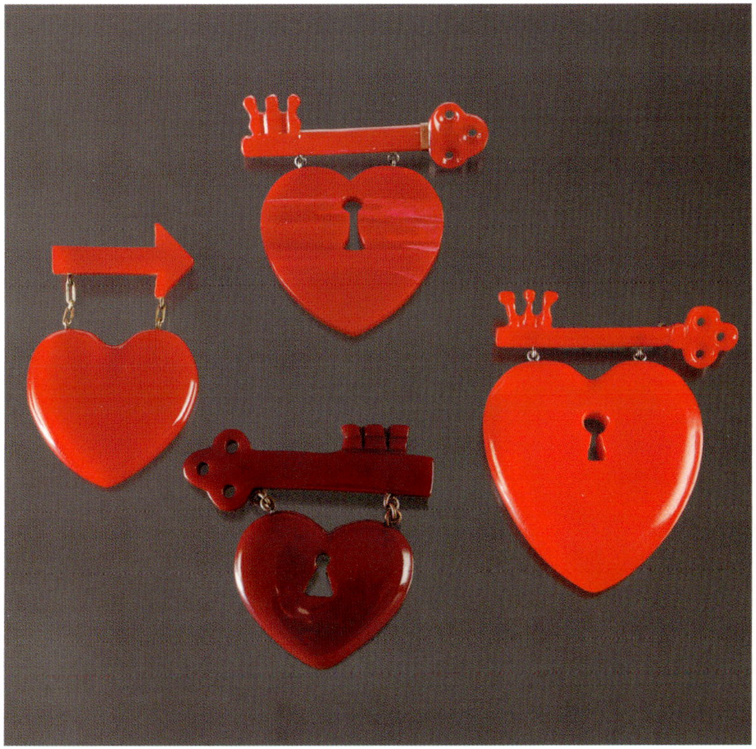

Four arrow or key bar pins, each with a red heart suspended

Red heart pin with golden metal "Sweetheart" applied

Arrow bar pin with a red heart suspended

CHAPTER 5

SWEETHEARTS

Four red arrow or key bar pins, each with a red heart suspended

Key bar pin
with a red heart
suspended

Red heart pin
with golden metal
"Sweetheart" applied

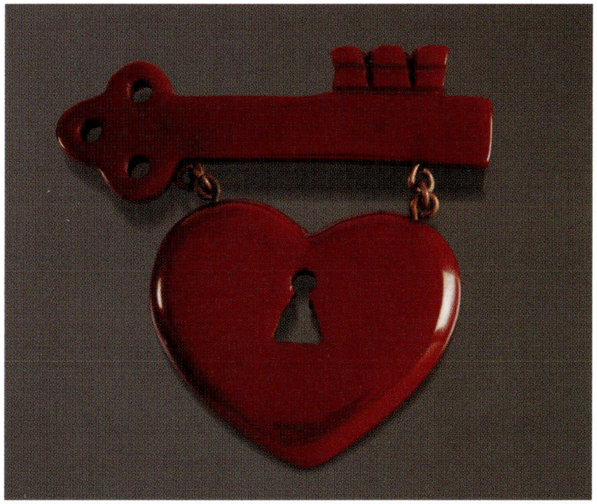

Large Dark Red Heart and Key Pin.

CHAPTER 5

SWEETHEARTS

Arrow bar pins with a red heart suspended

Life magazine cover for April 28, 1941, "Red Is Right" and the pin shown in the previous image. The pin is from the author's collection.

The April 28,1941, issue of *Life Magazine* depicted a woman wearing a red Bakelite heart pin, dubbed "MacArthur's Heart."

Bar pin with "Victory Garden" with pendant charms of cherries, celery and carrot

VICTORY GARDEN

During the war, gardens were a much-needed response to food shortages. Growing your own food during WWII was a patriotic gesture known as keeping a "Victory Garden". All over the USA people in cities grew food, including on the lawns of government buildings and on rooftops.

Bar pin with "Victory Garden" with pendant charms of cherries, celery and carrot

Marbleized brown gardening hat with cherries pin

flower pot necklace, designed by Martha Sleeper

Martha Sleeper's yellow flower pin Large

Bar pin with "Victory Garden" with pendant charms of cherries, celery and carrot

Martha Sleeper's
yellow flower pin

Large carved, creamed corn colored, gardening hat pin with carrots

Tortoise shell colored link Victory Garden necklace with five vegetable and seed pack charms

Tortoise shell colored link Victory Garden necklace with five vegetable and seed pack charms

Large carved, creamed corn colored, gardening hat pin with carrots

Necklace of brown link chain and six vegetable tray charms

Green link necklace with four linked flower bouquets

Red link necklace with four 'V' for Victory links and seed packets

Large Martha Sleeper-designed wooden pin in the form of an open matchbook

LOVE TOKENS:

CANDY AND CIGARETTES

CHAPTER 7

CANDY AND CIGARETTES

Cigarette and matches bar pin, designed by Martha Sleeper and featured in a national Camels cigarette advertisement

Martha Sleeper's design for a necklace with tortoise shell translucent links and charms of three cigarettes, six matchsticks, and four cigarette packs

Small boxes of Camel cigarettes, along with matches, were sent to soldiers overseas in ration boxes. Giving cigarettes was considered an appropriate token of love.

Martha Sleeper's design for a red link necklace with charms representing five cigarettes and twelve matchsticks

Martha Sleeper's design for a woven cord necklace with pendants of six cigarettes and five assorted cigarette packs

Cigarette and matches bar pin, designed by Martha Sleeper

CHAPTER 7

CANDY AND CIGARETTES

Martha Sleeper's design for a cord necklace with pendants of four cigarettes and five connected matchsticks

Martha Sleeper's design for a link necklace with four Lucky Strike packs, five cigarettes and five matchsticks

CHAPTER 7

CANDY AND CIGARETTES

Large Martha Sleeper-designed wooden pin in the form of an open matchbook

Martha Sleeper's design for a large matchstick necklace on a metal back chain

Red arrow bar pin with dangling red heart and metal "Sweetheart" and anchor with coiled rope insignia

AS AMERICAN AS CHERRY PIE

Ten cherries with leaves on a cord necklace

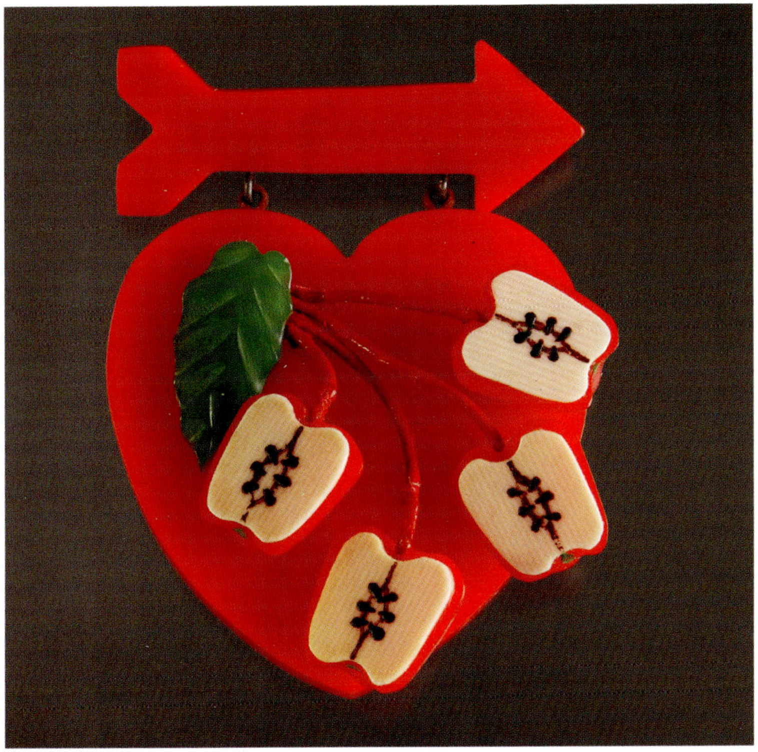

Large red heart pin with halved apples and an arrow bar

Red cherries on a brown log pin

"Don't sit under the apple tree with anyone else but me....till I come marching home." These lyrics were featured in a song in the Abbott and Costello film *Buck Privates*, and was recorded by the Andrews Sisters singers. The song was written by Lew Brown, Sam Sept, and Charlie Tobias to lift the spirits of the allied troops.

Small pin of five cherries on a log

Small pin of two cherries with leaves on a branch

Small pin of five cherries on a log

Pin of six cherries on a branch

Striped bar pin with a pendant red heart, "Waiting is the pits!" and two cherries with a leaf attached

Extra-large necklace of five pairs of carved and split cherries with leaves

Cord necklace with eight cherries and five leaves

MISSING CAPTION 08-010

Pin with a red heart and a cherry blossom with two leaves and two cherries

THE WEARING OF IDEAS

The Allies would use every resource possible to get their message out. Victory, we must! So what we experienced was the blatant use of symbolism in the Bakelite jewelry – iconographic jewelry – the wearing of ideas. Iconography, wearing bombs instead of roses on your lapel. It was modernism which introduced abstraction, i.e. geometric art deco design of the 30s, a real contrast with the organic beauty of the Beaux Arts movement, which was experienced in the previous decade. That transition is beautifully seen in Macintosh's art and architecture. The freedom of the 1930s abstraction, made a break with the naturalistic, allowed women to wear icons. This decoration with icons became a standard in American culture to this day where political pins express ideologies and through t-shirts and jewelry, can be relatively disturbing, i.e. safety pins.

Americans lives changed with women playing a major role in the war effort. Remember Rosie the Riveter? Rosie was the cultural icon of the United States representing the American women who worked in factories during World War II. American women took over manufacturing jobs in industry as well as becoming bus, streetcar and taxi drivers. Not only were women in the military, they were in the factories, many support services and at home, waiting.

Women's roles changed dramatically with the War. The USO was developed to lend support to our troops. Navy Nurses served on Navy hospital ships in the Pacific Ocean. The women's army corps packed parachutes. Patriotic jobs were done out of love. Because of the need for metals in the war effort, Bakelite jewelry became more popular out of practicality and patriotism. Women drew lines up their legs with pencils instead of wearing nylons. In the United States women were encouraged to be frugal which included the practice of rationing.

There were the WACS: Women's Army Corps and the WASPs: Women's Air force Service Pilots. Ever heard of Tokyo Rose? Most commonly associated with the title was Iva Toguri, an American stranded in Japan after the outbreak of the war who was forced to broadcast propaganda to the Allied troops via the radio. We are not only talking about With urgency to win the war, the message had to be clear and strength in numbers was imperative. Certainly the Bakelite Jewelry was fashion forward, but with a purpose. This was also the beginning in mass marketing, sometimes in the form of propaganda. Iconographic jewelry–the wearing of ideas–included wearing bombs instead of roses on your lapel. Decoration with icons became a standard in American culture to this day, where political pins express ideologies.

The 1940s was also a time when Canadian women played a huge role in the war effort, as well as women from Australia.

Bakelite jewelry kits were sold in "five-and-dime" stores in the 1930s and '40s. Artists commissioned factories to execute their designs in the same way jewelers do today. Charms were designed by an artist, manufactured, and distributed through newspapers.

Martha Sleeper is the most recognized designer of Bakelite jewelry to collectors today. She is responsible for first introducing the idea of whimsy into the jewelry. Sleeper's work can be seen as a prototype for contemporary pop(ular) culture. It is no surprise that American artist Andy Warhol was an avid collector of Bakelite Jewelry.

Belle Kogan was one of the first industrial designers to experiment with plastics, and her designs were made throughout the Bakelite era. Many well-known design houses employed Ms. Kogan for her visionary designs in plastics as an introduction to the commercial market. In the late 1930s, Ms. Kogan was a founding member of the New York Chapter of the American Designer's Institute, which later evolved into the Industrial Designers Institute. Ms. Kogan received the personal Recognition Award in 1994 from the Industrial Society of America.

Today, the influence of these designers is seen in works by contemporary artists such as Cara Croninger, another pioneer in the use of resins in art jewelry. Ms Croninger is still active in her New York City studio, working with resins as a visual artist. Hers were among of the original "sculptures to wear" as an art movement. Her influence was recognized at most high fashion department stores and in the collections of many commercial artists of the day. Cara Croninger's modern application of resin makes her one of the most respected artists of the century.

ORIGINS OF BAKELITE

ORIGINS OF

CHAPTER 10

BAKELITE

Bakelite was the first man-made resin, produced by Dr. Leo Baekeland (1863-1944), a Belgian chemist living and working in New York state. He came to America as an immigrant from Ghent, Belgium, where his father was a shoemaker and his mother a maid. He achieved recognition at the University of Bruges, where he was a professor, and developed a passion for photography and chemistry while at University. In 1889, at the age of 26, Baekeland received a scholarship to travel with his wife to the United States. At the age of 36, Baekeland made the discovery of a synthetic resin, and refined it during his experiments from 1907 to 1909.

Dr. Baekeland pressure-mixed two chemicals, formaldehyde and carbolic acid. Earlier resins, like celluloid, were extremely flammable and there existed the need for a safer material. Bakelite was used originally as an insulator. The General Bakelite Company, later re-named Bakelite Corporation, opened in 1910 to manufacture thermosetting plastic. The first Bakelite was used for industrial purposes, but when the original patent for phenyl-formaldehyde resin expired in 1927, other manufacturers made the material as well. Bakelite was used for many purposes, including radio housings, clocks, and household items such as doorknobs, kitchen knives and toasters. The name Bakelite is a trade name for the Bakelite Corporation. Bake-a-lite is the way the Baekeland family would like the word to be pronounced.

Originally popular for consumer goods in the 1920s to 1940s, Bakelite regained popularity in the 1980s for jewelry. A new generation discovered the Bakelite forms created during the early 20th century. A resurgence of the Bakelite market exists today.

In 1924, *Time Magazine* featured Leo Baekeland on the cover of an issue, and later declared him one of the outstanding chemists of the 20th century. He was one of the first chemists to be inducted into the National Inventors Hall of Fame, in Akron Ohio, along with Charles Goodyear. His invention of Bakelite impacted industrial products in a way no one could have possibly imagined.

Martha Sleeper loved working with her hands. As demand for her Bakelite jewelry designs grew, she would design a piece and have it assembled by workers. She had contracts with manufacturers for a line of jewelry bearing her label. Ms. Sleeper considered herself an artist. Her "Martha Sleeper" label sold the jewelry with whimsical designs. She had an outrageous sense of humor.

The market today for Bakelite jewelry of the 1940s is strong. Serious collectors build their collections through private, knowledgeable dealers. There are several good books about Bakelite jewelry, and now blogs and web sites that cover them adequately and are readily available. Mathew Burkholz addresses issues of authenticity in his book, *The Bakelite Collection*, as do several others.

Recommended Reading

Following is a list of suggested reading material about Bakelite jewelry as a collectible and a cultural manifestation. Also listed are a few wonderful books on the subject of World War Two.

"Bakelite Envy." *Connoisseur,* July 1985.

Bell, C. Jeanenne. *Answers to Questions About Old Jewelry:1840-1950.* Americana Publishing, 4th ed.,1996.

Burkholz, Mathew L., *The Bakelite Collection.* Atglen, Pennsylvania: Schiffer Publishing Ltd.,1997.

Dinato, Andrea.*Women Designers of the USA: Diversity and Difference 1900-2000.*Yale University Press, 2002.

"Googley Eye Pumpkin Pin." Morphy Auctions 12/08; catalogue available online; morphyauctions.com

Lockery, A.J. *Plastics in the Home and School Workshop.* London: Van Nostrand and Company, 1940.

Kelly, Lyngerde and Nancy Schiffer. *Plastic Jewelry.* Atglen, Pennsylvania: Schiffer Publishing Ltd, 1987.

Kitchens, James H. and Bernard, C. Nulty. *Flying Aces, Aviation Art of WWII.* New York: Metro Books, 2002.

Reboul, Percy and Rob Perree. *Bakelite: The Material of A Thousand Uses.* Cadre,1996.

Stolley, Bullfinch. *Life: World War 2: History's Greatest Conflict in Pictures.* Boston, New York and London: Little Brown and Company.

Ward, Geoffry C. and Ken Burns. *The War: An Intimate History 1941-1945.* New York: Knopf, 2007.

The National World War II Museum. New Orleans, Louisiana. An excellent resource and a very special place to visit.

www.icons.org.uk/theicons/collection/white-cliffs-of-dover/comments

www.IDSA.org/Bellekogan

www.jilldaniels.com/white-cliffs-dover-chords.

www.militaryhistoryonline.com

Husband